Table of Contents

Chapter 1: Introduction 4

Chapter 2: What Are Musical Notes? 7

Chapter 3: The Fretboard 11

Chapter 4: Getting To Know The Open Strings 15

Chapter 5: Getting Familiar With The Notes On The E and A Strings 21

Chapter 6: Fretboard Memorization Exercises 38

Chapter 7: Practice Routine Ideas 64

Chapter 8: Conclusion 71

Chapter 1: Introduction

Having the fretboard memorized with the ability to recall the location of notes at any given time, is a skill that can benefit all kinds of guitar players, regardless of skill level. Though the idea of "fretboard memorization" may seem inherently simple, it is both useful and relevant to all guitarists.

Here are just a few of the reasons why you might benefit from memorizing the fretboard:

- The fretboard will seem less intimidating when you improvise or learn your notes *(improvising is creating and playing a melody, solo, or chord progression, whether alone or with a band, without having any sheet music or tablature in front of you)*.
- It helps us to emphasize and create tonal changes within our melodies, solos, and chords.
- It allows us to get a better grasp on scales, as we learn the different kinds.
- It allows you to break free from regular open chords and barre chords so that you can locate smaller, more intricate chord voicings.

Guitar Fretboard:

A Quick & Simple Guide to Memorizing the Fretboard

By: Gary Nelson

Copyright © 2021

ALL RIGHTS RESERVED

No part of this book may be reproduced, stored in a retrieval system, or transmitted in any form or by any means, electronic, mechanical, photocopying, recording, scanning, or otherwise, without the prior written permission of the publisher.

Limit of Liability/Disclaimer of Warranty: the publisher and the author make no representations or warranties with respect to the accuracy or completeness of the contents of this work and specifically disclaim all warranties, including without limitation warranties of fitness for a particular purpose. No warranty may be created or extended by sales or promotional materials. The advice and strategies contained herein may not be suitable for every situation. This work is sold with the understanding that the publisher is not engaged in rendering medical, legal, or other professional advice or services. If professional assistance is required, the services of a competent professional person should be sought. Henceforth, neither the publisher nor the author shall be liable for any damages that may arise. The fact that an individual, organization or website is referred to in this work as a citation and/or potential source of further information does not mean that the author or the publisher endorses the information the individuals, organization or website may provide or recommendations they/it may make. Further, readers should be aware that websites listed on this work may have changed or disappeared between when this work was written and when it is read.

With that being said, we are going to assume that you are taking your first steps into the world of guitar at this moment and have little or no knowledge of the guitar or the concepts that surround it.

1.1 - Getting Started

Thank you for choosing our fretboard memorization book! The concepts and techniques that we've put together are here to help you move closer towards your goal as a great guitarist!

To get you started, there are a few guitar parameters that you need to have an understanding of:

- A standard guitar has anywhere from 21-24 frets
- A standard guitar has six strings, ordered from lowest to highest in pitch
- Each fret represents a movement of one half-step within the 12 notes of the western musical alphabet

As you venture further into this book, take note that we are not providing you with exercises, playing techniques, or lessons on general music theory. Instead, this book is purely intended for developing mental recall of the fretboard through visualization and memorization techniques.

One of the *most* important things to develop when memorizing the fretboard is something we like to call *spatial awareness.*

1.2 - Spatial Awareness

Spatial awareness is the idea of focusing on the visual relationship between the fretboard of the guitar and the musical alphabet. Whether you have your guitar with you or not, you should be able to practice the methods we discuss in this book.

Remember to take things slow.

One of the biggest struggles for new guitarists is the desire to quickly become an expert. Unfortunately, speed and efficiency are not always friends when it comes to learning any instrument. We advise you to take things slow: be sure that you have a good grasp of the techniques we are discussing in one section before moving on to the next section.

Chapter 2: What Are Musical Notes?

Now, before we get into fretboard memorization techniques, let's make sure that you have a decent understanding of musical notes.

A musical note shows the pitch and duration of a sound.

2.1 - The Pitch Of A Musical Note

Pitch is how **high** or **low** a note sounds. Sound is made up of waves, or vibrations, which occur at different speeds. If the frequency or speed of a wave vibrates faster, then the pitch of that note will be higher.

This is why the thinnest string on your guitar sounds higher in pitch than the thickest string on your guitar.

2.2 - Understanding Musical Scales

While we don't want to get too deep into scales in this book, it is worth talking about them briefly so that you have an idea of the notes we're talking about.

We've got specific pitches in music that make up our standard notes. The chromatic scale, which is a series of 12 notes that ascend or descend in half-step increments, is an important scale for all musicians to know. Essentially, the scale helps us to name every note on the fretboard of the guitar, one by one, in succession.

The notes in the chromatic scale look a little like this:

C	C#/Db	D	D#/Eb	E	F	F#/Gb	G	G#/Ab	A	A#/Bb	B	C

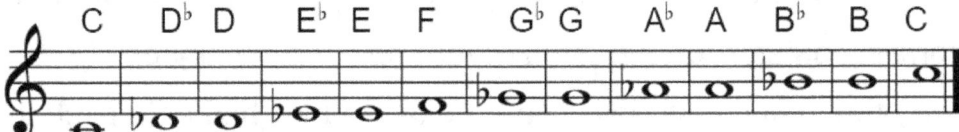

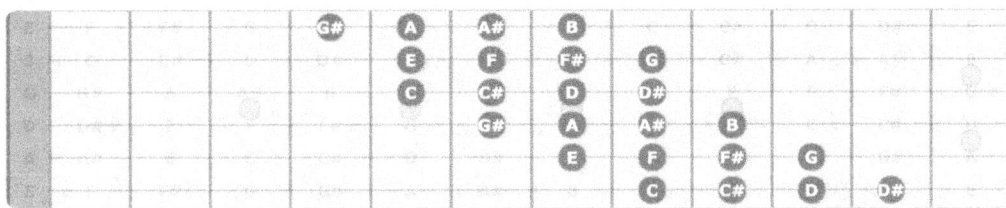

The seven **natural** notes in typically western music are **C, D, E, F, G, A, B**.

The small "#" and "♭" symbols (sharp and flat, respectively) that you see between the notes are known as **accidentals**.

Put the seven natural notes and the accidentals in the right order, and you will have the **12 possible notes** of the chromatic scale.

As you can see from the diagrams above, this chromatic sequence starts on the note **C** and ends on the note **C**, one octave higher.

Like we said earlier, we can think of the chromatic scale as a way of moving up and down the series of musical notes in the smallest possible increments. A sharp (#) is one half-step up from a natural note, while A flat (♭) is one half-step down from a natural note.

Depending on the musical context, these altered notes can either be seen as sharp notes or flat notes.

For example, the half-step increment between notes F and G can either be referred to as **F#** or **G♭**. These are what we call "enharmonic notes," meaning they sound the same, though are written differently. Typically, sharps are used when ascending, while flats are used while descending. So, if we went **up** a half step from F, we would call that note **F#**. On the contrary, if we went **down** a half step from G, we would call that note **G♭**.

As you can see in the diagrams, there are two exceptions to the sharps and flats between natural notes: the space between **B-C,** and between **E-F**. These notes are *already* a half-step apart, so there is no need to put a sharp or flat between them.

It is very important that you have an understanding of how musical notes are ordered before we get into the rest of the book. As you'll soon find out, the notes on the guitar are laid out in a similar fashion to the chromatic scale.

Chapter 3: The Fretboard

3.1 - The Layout of the Fretboard

Now that you have a good understanding of notes in the chromatic scale, let's now turn our focus to the fretboard of the guitar.

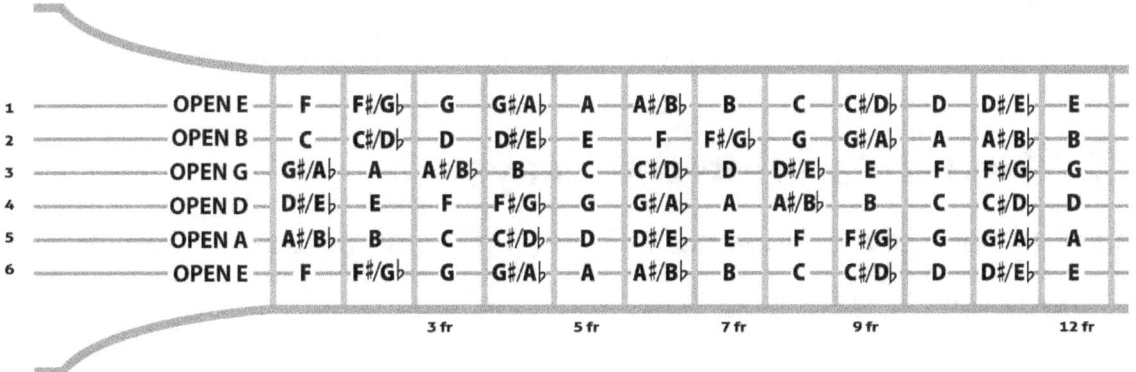

The fretboard, sometimes called the fingerboard, is the top part of the guitar neck that sits between the body and the headstock.

If you look at the diagram above, you will see all of the notes on the fretboard from each open string to the 12th fret. We stopped at the 12th fret because the notes on the fretboard repeat themselves after the 12th fret.

*For example, you can see that the note **F** is on the first fret of the E string above. This means that the note **F** will also be on the thirteenth fret of the E string.*

Yes, we know that this looks like a lot of notes, and you may be thinking, "how could anyone possibly memorize all of this?"

The guitar layout does not seem as obvious when compared to the piano. The cool thing is, there are reference points on the guitar's fretboard that *become* obvious once we get deeper into it.

3.2 - Understanding the Inlays

Inlays are one of the fundamental elements of the fretboard. They are key when it comes to visualizing notes on the fretboard.

The inlays are decorative elements set into the exterior wood on both electric and acoustic guitars. Inlays can be customized with all different types of shapes and materials to give the guitars a unique and visually appealing look.

While inlays are used on various parts of the instrument, including the body and headstock, we are *specifically* talking about the inlays on the fretboard.

Of course, inlays aren't just here for decoration.

They serve a unique and helpful purpose: to guide us with our positioning on the neck. In fact, inlays are one of the most helpful tools for guitarists who are learning to navigate and memorize the fretboard.

Inlays are installed using well-thought-out patterns. Depending on the guitar manufacturer, the shapes can vary from large blocks, small dots, diamonds, and more exotic designs. For the most part, fretboard inlays will mark the odd-numbered frets while skipping the 11th fret and marking the 12th, or the octave.

While inlay patterns can vary, especially on classical guitars, you will typically see this pattern:

- **Single inlays** on the **3rd, 5th, 7th, 9th, 15th, 17th, 19th,** and **21st** frets, while **double inlays** on the **12th** and **24th** frets. Of course, some guitars have less than 24 frets, so it depends on your guitar.

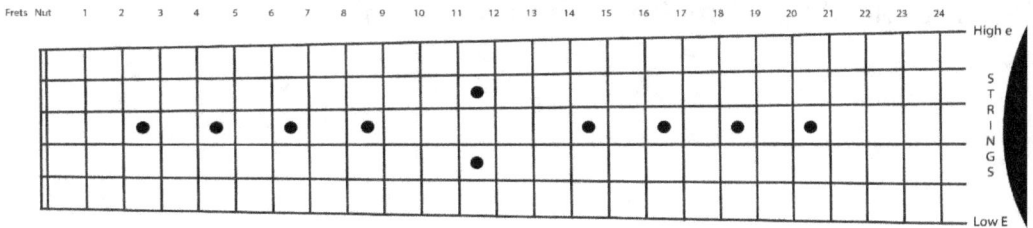

To keep things simple, we will be using the most popular pattern as a reference throughout our book (shown above).

Before we get any deeper into the notes of our fretboard, take a minute to memorize the location of the inlays on your fretboard.

Looking at your guitar, you should notice some symmetry from the **1st-12th** fret and the **12th-24th** fret. *For example, we can see that there is an inlay on the **3rd fret**. The note found on the third fret on any given string will also be found on the **15th fret** of that same string, as it is three frets above the octave.*

Hopefully you are now feeling a bit more comfortable with the frets. The inlays help us to visualize the fretboard in sections so that we don't have to be overwhelmed by memorizing the whole neck of the guitar.

We will use the inlays as reference points throughout this book. Remember, it is only necessary to memorize the notes from the **1st-12th** fret, as the pattern repeats itself from the **12th** fret onwards.

Chapter 4: Getting To Know The Open Strings

Understanding your open strings is the first step in memorizing the fretboard.

We will be using the open strings to talk about our finger placement on the guitar.

So what are the open strings of the guitar?

First String	E (Thinnest)
Second String	B
Third String	G
Fourth String	D
Fifth String	A
Sixth String	E (Thickest)

Mnemonic devices are often used to help us recall information easily. They also aid in learning how to memorize musical elements. Here are a few mnemonic devices to help you with the open strings:

4.1 - From Thin (high e) To Thick (low E)

- **E**very **B**oy **G**ets **D**izzy **A**round **E**lle
- **E**aster **B**unny **G**ets **D**runk **A**fter **E**aster

4.2 - From Thick (low E) To Thin (high e)

- **E**ddie **A**te **D**ynamite, **G**ood **B**ye **E**ddy
- **E**aster **A**ngels **D**on't **G**ive **B**roken **E**ggs

Of course, these are just a few that we've learned along the way. You are more than welcome to make up your own if that helps! It's common to memorize the strings from low **E** to high **e**, but whichever direction is comfortable for you, it's the one you should use.

The reason these devices are so helpful is that they use the notes of the open strings moving from the highest to lowest, or lowest to highest strings (vertically).

4.3 - Tones and Semitones

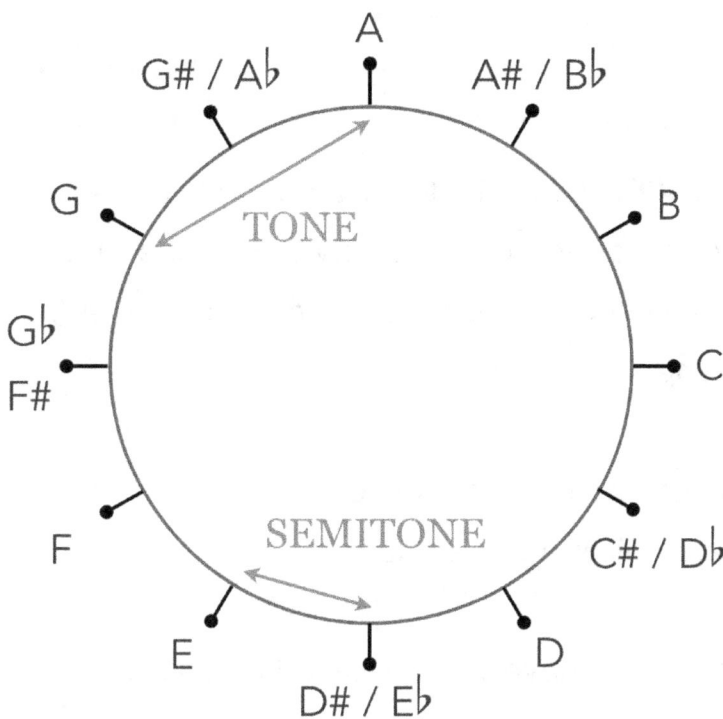

Look at the diagram above, and you will see the series of notes moving clockwise around the circle in order.

Each step around this circle of notes is representative of a **semitone**.

We can see these same notes arranged on the fretboard diagram below:

The step from **D#/Eb** up to **E,** for example, is one semitone and is the distance of one fret on the guitar. Every fret on the guitar is equal to one semitone. You will often hear semitones referred to as a "half-steps," which are the same thing.

If you move up one fret or down one fret on any given string, you are moving up or down one **semitone** or **half-step**.

On the other hand, we have what is called a **tone**, which equals two half-steps, or two frets on the guitar. For example, the movement from **G** up to **A** is a **tone** since we move from **G** to **G#/Ab,** then to **A**. You will often hear tones referred to as "**whole-steps**."

Now, try this out on your guitar!
Put your finger down on any fret and play the next fret above. This is what a semitone (half-step) sounds like. *Do you recognize this sound? Do you know songs or melodies that have this sound?*

Now put your finger on the same fret, but this time move *two* steps up. This is what a tone (whole-step) sounds like. *Where do you recognize this sound from?*

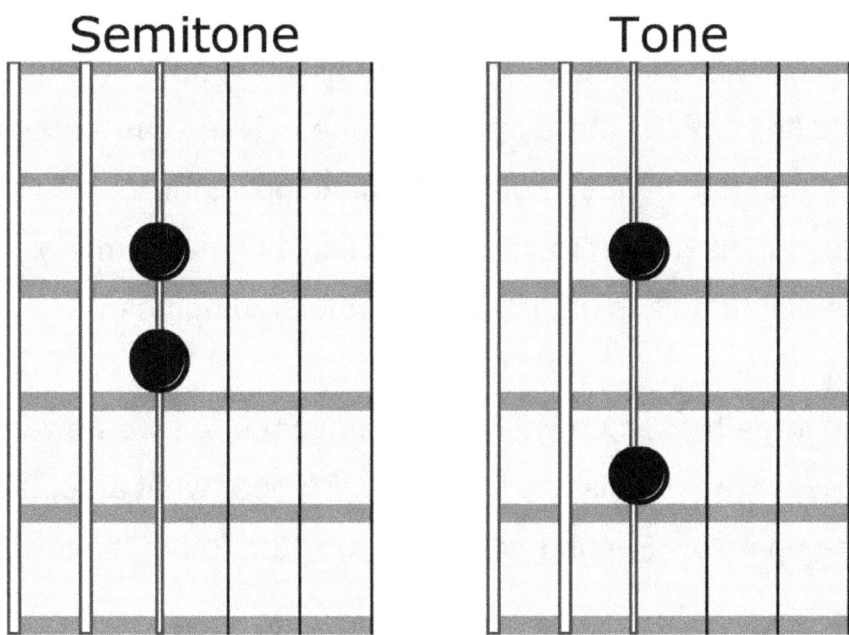

Tones and semitones will come up in our later chapters, so it is essential that you have a good grasp of them now!

4.4 - The Importance of the Octave

By now, you should have understood that the chromatic scale, common in Western music, uses seven unique notes with accidentals in-between them (12 semitones in all).

So what happens after those 12 notes?

The twelfth note, known as the **octave**, is the end of the scale. Once we hit the twelfth note from where we started, we begin the scale all over again.

The octave is simply the distance between the first note in your series and the last (twelfth) note in the chromatic series. The term "octave" actually hints at the number 8 (the prefix **oct** meaning eight, of course); this is because, in our most common musical scales (major, minor, all Greek modes), the eighth note is an octave from the starting note.

An octave can be broken down into 12 semitones. As we now know, each fret on the guitar represents one semitone. To hear what an octave sounds like, play the open low E string, then play the 12th fret of the low E string.

You will notice that the 12th fret of the low E string is *also* the note **E**, though it is an octave higher.

Fun Fact: *When you play a note an octave higher, you are doubling the rate at which the frequency vibrates.*

As of now, it is vital that you understand what an octave is because octaves are one of the most important tools for memorizing the fretboard, as you will see later in this book.

Chapter 5: Getting Familiar With The Notes On The E and A Strings

By now, you should have a good understanding of the fretboard layout. In this chapter, we are going to dive deeper into various spots on the fretboard to gain a better understanding of the notes along its entirety.

For beginners, the notes on the **E** and **A** strings will be the most important notes to learn and memorize. This is because the notes found on these two strings are the most common notes used in movable chord shapes.

Once you have the notes on the **E** and **A** strings down, the rest of this book will seem like a piece of cake. That is because this section is where pure memorization occurs.

While we're going to touch other strings, as they are as well important, we won't have to use the same memorization techniques on all strings. The notes on the **E** and **A** strings are simply a foundation for our patterns, which we will discuss in later chapters.

Let's start with the thickest and most important string, the **E** string.

5.1 - E String

We know that our open **E** string is the natural note **E**.

Now, if we refer back to the chromatic scale, we can see that the next note up from the open **E** string, which is on our **1st** fret, is the natural note **F**. While we do not have an inlay here on the **1st** fret to help us, it is useful to memorize that this is where our **F** is.

Now let's move to the inlay on the third fret, a tone (whole-step) up from the first fret (**F**), which is the natural note **G**.

We can continue moving up on our inlays to get to the **5th**, **7th**, and **9th** frets, which are **A, B,** and **C#/Db**, respectively.

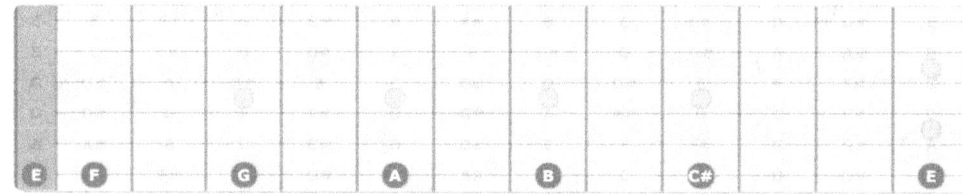

E String

You can use this helpful mnemonic device, to memorize these notes:

Fat **G**oat **A**te **B**ig **C**ookie

Keep this mnemonic device in your back pocket, and you'll find out that memorizing the names of the notes will be easier than ever.

As you can see, we have the **C#/Db** on the **9th** fret, which may look a little strange considering that the rest of the notes on the inlays are natural. In addition, you have to move three frets up from the **9th** fret to get to the **12th** fret or octave, which makes things a bit harder to memorize.

Because of this, we like to provide guitarists with an *alternative* option for memorizing the notes on these strings. Instead of thinking of the **9th** fret as **C#/Db**, think of it as the fret *between* two frets with natural notes:

- **C** on the **8th** fret
- **D** on the **10th** fret

E String

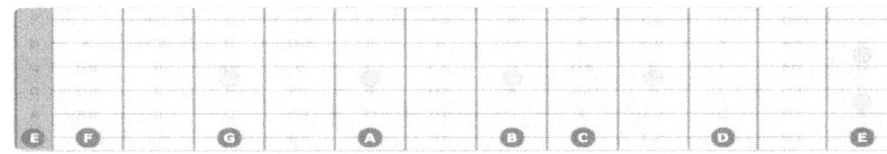

If you want, you can even change the mnemonic device slightly to fit this pattern:

Fat **G**oat **A**te **B**ig **C**orn **D**og

Ready for the best part?

Do you remember how the **low E** string and the **high** string have the same notes? Once you have the **low E** string down, you would have also memorized the **high e** string!

Essentially, we've just killed two birds with one stone! Check it out:

E String

All you have to do here is memorize the location of these **seven notes**. The beauty here is that they are in alphabetical order; the only exception is that the musical alphabet stops at the note **G,** then moves to **A,** and then the series continues alphabetically.

Now that you are comfortable and confident with the **E** string, let's move on to the **A** string.

5.2 - A String

We can use the same methods that we just used with the **E** string to locate our notes on the **A** string.

The only difference is that this time, instead of relying on the inlays, we will use our knowledge of tones and semitones because this will help us construct a series of natural notes, rather than a series of accidental notes. We will first start with the open string, which is the note **A**.

We can move up two semitones (one tone) from there to get to our natural note **B** on the **2nd** fret. From there, we can move one semitone up to get to our natural note **C** on the **3rd** fret, which is marked with an inlay.

We can also move up two semitones (one tone) to the inlay on the **5th** fret to get our natural note **D** and two more semitones (one tone) up to our inlay on the **7th** fret to get our natural note **E**.

Now, while our next instinct might be to hit that inlay on the **9th** fret, we will refrain from doing so. If we do move up to the **9th** fret, we create the same issue that we had when we looked for the note on the **9th** fret of the **E** string.

*Instead of the note **F**, which we want to find next on the **A** string, we will find **F#/Gb** on the **9th** fret.*

Instead, we will go up one semitone from the natural note **E** on the **7th** fret to get to our natural note **F** on the **8th** fret. From there, we can move two semitones (one tone) up to **G** on the **10th** fret, and finally, **A** on the **12th** fret, to resolve our octave

A String

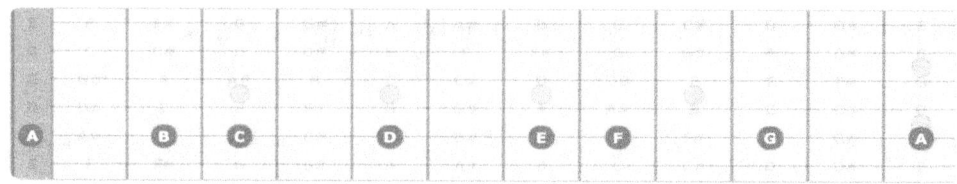

Here is a mnemonic device to help you memorize these notes:

Big **C**ats **D**on't **E**at **F**resh **G**rapes

Remember, our mnemonic devices were made to help us and others, though they are not set in stone. Feel free to create a custom mnemonic device for yourself if you can think of something better!

5.3 - Sharps and Flats On The E and A Strings

Now that we have an understanding of the majority of the notes found on the **E** and **A** strings, let's begin filling in some of the missing pieces. The best way to do this is to use our knowledge of tones (whole-steps) and semitones (half-steps) to figure out the notes that are left.

For example, if we are on the **E** string, and we want to find the note **F#**, it is as simple as moving up from the natural note **F**, which we already know is on the first fret.

We find our **F#** when we move up one semitone (half-step) from our natural note **F**, as seen below:

Of course, we don't *only* move **up** when using tones and semitones; we can also move down!

This means that you could start with your natural note **G** when looking for **F#**, and instead of moving a semitone up, you move a semitone down.

In this case, however, you would use the **enharmonic equivalent** of **F#**, which is **Gb**, to notate the interval. Remember, we use sharps when ascending (like **F** to **F#**) and flats when descending (like **G** to **Gb**).

We can use tones and semitones throughout the entirety of the fretboard to find the in-between notes or notes with accidentals. Check it out:

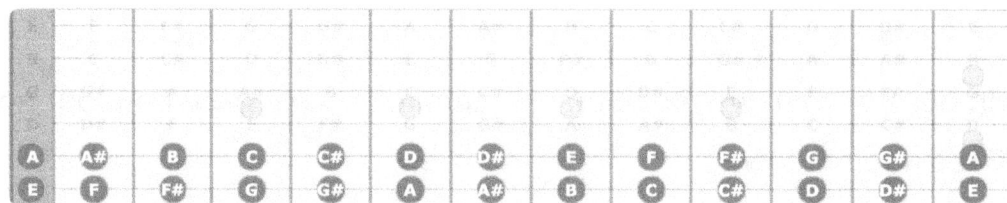

It is important to note that you actually have found all the notes for **THREE** strings rather than just the bottom two, as the **high e** string is a reflection of the **low E** string.

This is the only part of the book that requires pure memorization. From now on, we will be using helpful patterns to discover the other notes on the fretboard.

Before you move on, we recommend that you spend some time trying to get familiar with the notes on the **E** and **A** strings. Use your mnemonic devices to find your first pattern across the **E** and **A** strings, then use your knowledge of tones and semitones to fill in the missing notes.

5.4 - Finding Octaves From the E and A Strings

This is where things start to get exciting, as we will begin to unlock a few essential patterns to help us memorize the rest of the fretboard.

While there are many different "methods" that can be used to memorize the fretboard in its entirety, we have found out that there is one method that works best, time and time again.

That method is the **octave method.**

You should remember from our earlier chapters that an octave is simply two notes that are 12 semitones up or down from each other.

When you play an open string, you can find the octave of that open string on the 12th fret. The beauty of this is that there are other instances of the octave, which can help us create familiarity with other pitches throughout the length of the fretboard. The way that the fretboard is set up makes using the octave incredibly easy.

Now, there is some theory as to *why* we find octaves in certain places. The guitar is tuned mostly in perfect fourths from string to string, which enables our movements from one octave to the next. But, there is a simpler way to look at this.

Instead, we are going to use a simple shape to get us from our root to our octave.

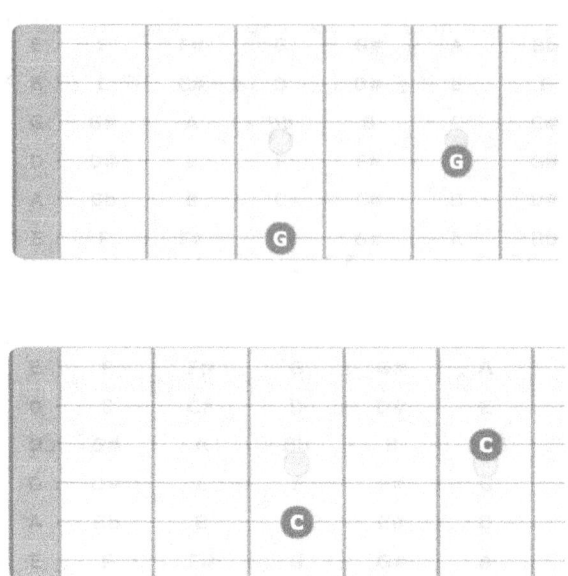

Take a look at the shapes above, and you will notice that, though they take place on different strings, they utilize the same pattern of **"up two strings, up two frets."**

In the first pattern, you can see that the **G** found on the sixth string (low **E**) has its octave two strings up and two frets up on the fourth string (**D**). The cool thing is that this works for all the notes above and below **G**!

Let's imagine that you are playing a note on the **D** string, and you are not sure what it is called; you can simply reverse this pattern: move two frets down and two strings down from that note to find its lower octave on the sixth string (low **E**).

Now, look at the second pattern with the natural note **C** on the third fret of the fifth string (**A**) and the fifth fret of the third string (**G**). You can use the exact same pattern here! *Up two strings, up two frets.*

Let's say you were on the fifth fret of the third (**G**) string, and you were unsure on the note you were on. You could simply reverse the process again: move two frets down and two strings down from that note to find your lower octave **C**.

Not only are these octave shapes helpful in terms of memorization, they are also easily playable. You can place your first finger on the lower octave and your third, or fourth, finger on the upper octave. Doing so can help you visualize your octaves a lot easier and create muscle memory as you move along the neck.

To help make things a bit easier to reference and memorize, here are the notes that are found on the fourth (**D**) string:

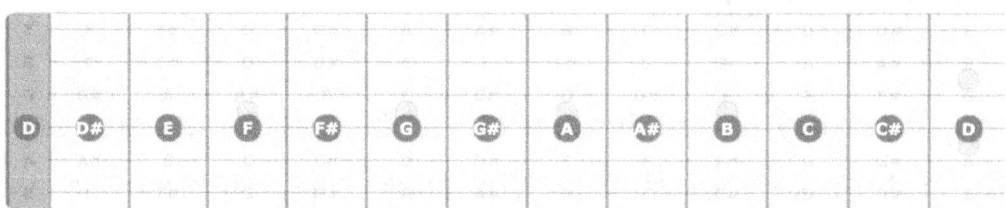

Here are the notes that are found on the third (**G**) string:

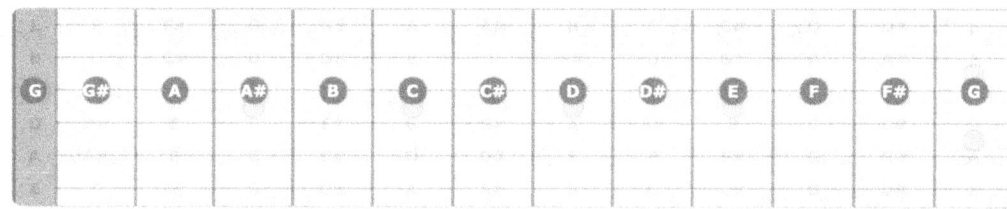

You've now made some serious progress!

By using our handy octave pattern from the **E** and **A** strings, we can *easily* locate notes on the **D** and **G** strings. At this point, you should have a good idea of the notes found on four strings of the guitar!

Pretty awesome, right?

Make sure that you take some time to memorize all of these octaves before moving on to the next section so that you have a solid grasp of these four strings.

5.5 - Finding Octaves From the D and G Strings

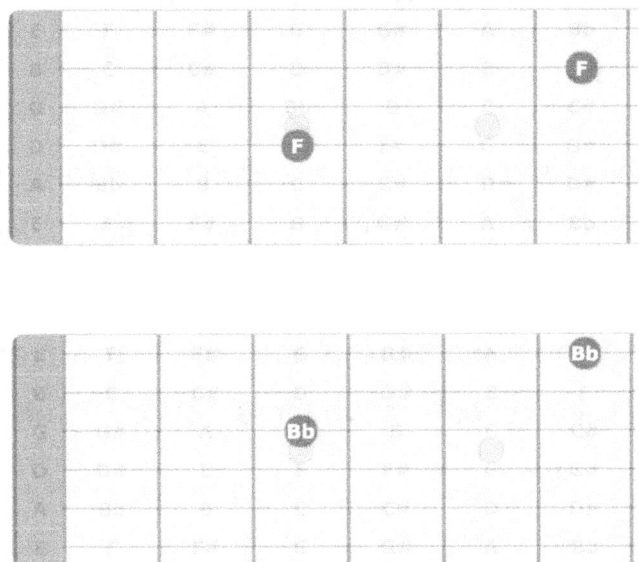

The octave relationships for the **D** and **G** strings are a bit different due to the unique tuning of the **B** string. The reason, which we won't get too deep into, is that the **B** string is tuned to a major third rather than a fourth like the rest of the strings on the guitar.

This means that we cannot use the same shape we used for the **E** and **A** strings to locate our octaves. We must adjust our shape to locate octaves on the **B** and **high e** strings.

Take a look at the diagram above.

It shows the relationship between the fourth string (**D**) and the second string (**B**). As you can see, instead of going two strings up and two frets up to find the octave from the **D** string, we are moving two strings up and **three** frets up.

The same method is used in the second diagram, which shows the relationship between the third string (**G**) and the first string (**high e**).

This means that if you are unsure of the note that you are on, on the **G** or **high e** strings, you can simply move three frets down and two strings down to find the lower octave.

5.6 - Alternative Octave Patterns

Some people find it easier to find octaves on the **B** and **high e** strings using their relationships with the **A** and **low E** strings.

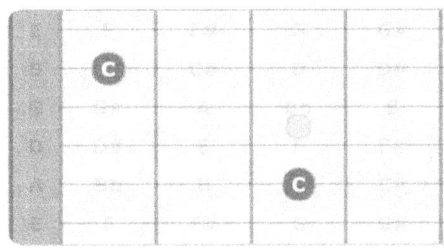

Let's start with the relationship between the **A** and **B** strings or the fifth and second strings.

The diagram above shows the octave relationship between the two strings. If you're familiar with your traditional open chords, you might realize that this is the outline of the C major chord in an open position.

Let's say you were on the first fret of the second (**B**) string, and that you were unsure of the note you were on. You could simply count two frets up and three strings down to get to the lower octave on the fifth (**A**) string.

This shape can be moved up the entire fretboard to help you find all the octaves between the fifth (**A**) and second (**B**) strings.

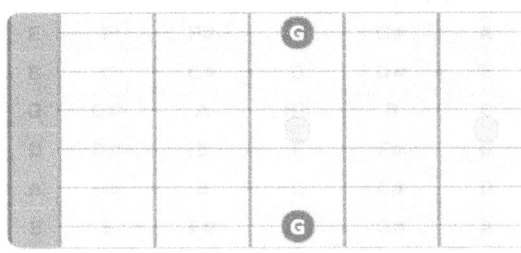

Now let's move on to the relationship between the sixth string (**low E**) and first string (**high e**).

As we know, these strings mirror one another.

If for example, you were on the third fret of the first string (**high e**) and you were unsure of the note, you could simply use your knowledge of the notes on the sixth string (**low E**) to figure out that it is a **G**.

The shape in the diagram above can be moved up the entire length of the fretboard to help you find the octave relationships between the two **E** strings.

*Note that the **E** strings are actually **two** octaves apart.*

Quick Exercise:

By now, you should have a good understanding of some of the different patterns found on the guitar. As an exercise, let's take a look at all the natural **C** notes found on the fretboard.

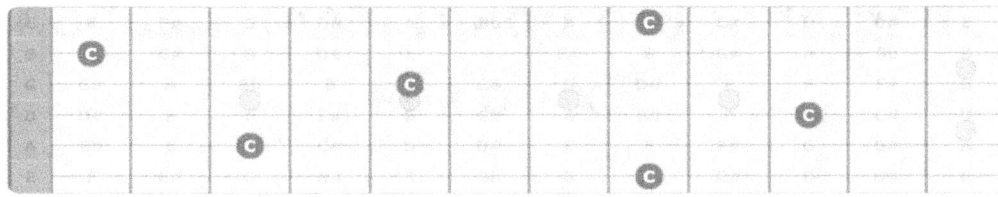

Take some time and visualize the octave patterns that we have just learned to move from one C to the next.

This exercise works for every note. It would be a great practice for you to pick any note and use your octave patterns to locate that same note on every string.

Congratulations!

At this point, you now have all the necessary tools to find any note on the fretboard!
That wasn't so hard, now was it?
Your best bet is to take a break at this point and process all of the octave patterns before moving on to our "Exercises" section.

If you make it a priority to process and memorize the octave patterns we have just gone through every day, you will be well on your way to mastering the fretboard.

Chapter 6: Fretboard Memorization Exercises

You should be proud of yourself!

You've come pretty far at this point.

We believe that now is the time to present you with some valuable exercises that can help you to further master your memorization abilities.

Remember, the ability to play the guitar in both fluid and intuitive manner requires physical and mental confidence. You must be aware of how your playing relates to the entire fretboard. This means that you need to be able to coordinate your movements between the frets and the strings.

Of course, there are likely **hundreds** of fretboard memorization exercises out in the ethos, though it would be quite overwhelming for anyone to go through all of them. In our opinion, the most beneficial exercises are the ones that focus on "spatial awareness."

As we discussed earlier, spatial awareness is the idea of looking for patterns through fret and string relationships on the guitar, as opposed solely memorizing note names. The exercises that we will present to you will create patterns which will feed your visual memory.

This allows us to learn the fretboard in a far more intuitive manner.

Let's start with one of our favorite ones…

6.1 - Vertical Anchor Points

When beginners attempt to locate notes on the fretboard, they typically use the method of counting through the musical alphabet on the open strings. The reason is that it is a familiar reference point for **all** guitarists. As long as you know the open strings, you can navigate to just about any note. However, this method becomes *far* less practical as you move further up the neck.

Luckily, there are a few alternative reference points to help us in this case. As we know, the open strings are fairly easy to memorize, since they don't contain any sharps or flats. What guitarists sometimes don't perceive is that there are other locations on the neck of the guitar where we can move from the highest to the lowest string without any sharps or flats.

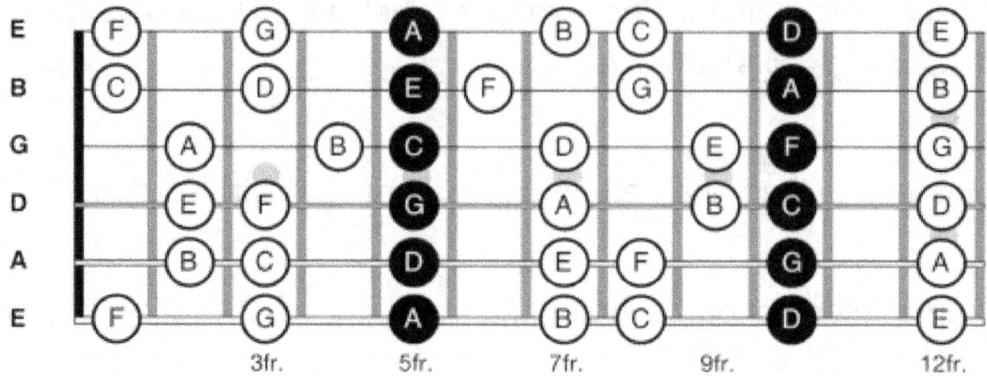

Moving beyond the open position, we can see that there are natural notes in vertical rows along the **fifth** and **tenth** frets. These rows are extremely convenient for fretboard memorization, as they are evenly spaced apart, giving us visual points of reference along the neck of the guitar.

*Remember how the notes repeat themselves after the 12th fret? This means that these **same series** of vertical notes appear on the 12th, 17th, and 22nd frets.*

We can use our new vertical anchor points on the **fifth** and **tenth** fret to craft an exercise.

You must start by memorizing the notes on the vertical anchor points. Once you have those memorized, we can use them to practice locating other notes along the chromatic scale.

For example, using the anchor points on the **fifth** fret, name the note on the seventh fret of the second string (**B**).

We know that **E** is the anchor point on the **fifth** fret of the second string, which means **F#** (two semitones up) is the note we're looking for.

Another example would be to name the note on the eleventh fret of the fifth string, using the anchor points on the **tenth** fret. We know that **G** is the anchor point on the **tenth** fret of the fifth string, which means **G#** (one semitone up) is the note we're looking for.

Use the anchor points on the **fifth** and **tenth** fret of each string and try to figure out the notes that surround them on either side. Make sure to spend the same amount of time with both anchor points to get an idea of the entire fretboard.

6.2 - Root Patterns

The **Root Patterns** exercise is helpful because it provides us with a way to identify and sequentially play any note anywhere on the fretboard. The root note is typically the starting note in a scale, a bass note in a chord, or tonic note in a key. Though, for this exercise, we will simply think of the root as our **starting point.**

Having an understanding of how notes move sequentially can help us to move along the neck without feeling hesitant.

There are many guitarists that work tirelessly to memorize every note of every string across the entire fretboard. While some are successful in doing so, others aren't, and this creates limitations when trying to play songs.

When you think of a series of notes as a pattern rather than individual notes, you begin to create a sense of spatial relativity. Your brain then develops muscle memory to help move your hands from one place to the next without hesitation to enable you stay in the moment with your music.

As an example, let's use the natural note **G**. As we discovered earlier, this note exists all over the fretboard.

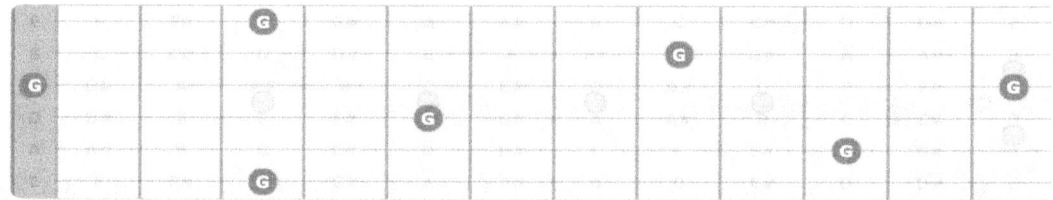

The goal of this root pattern exercise is to be able to pick any starting root position and immediately know where the root note lives in the other parts of the neck in the proximity of the root.

One of the best ways to do this is to look at patterns. Note that all of the patterns we are about to show you are completely movable. This means that no matter what note you are using as your root, all of these patterns will work.

The diagram below shows the relationship of every note **G** on the fretboard. Notice how they exist in different proximities of one another.

For example, we can use our octave patterns from Chapter 5, section 4. Let's say we have our **G** on the sixth string. If we want to find a **G** on the fourth string, we have to move two strings up and two frets over. This works for all note relationships between the sixth and fourth strings.

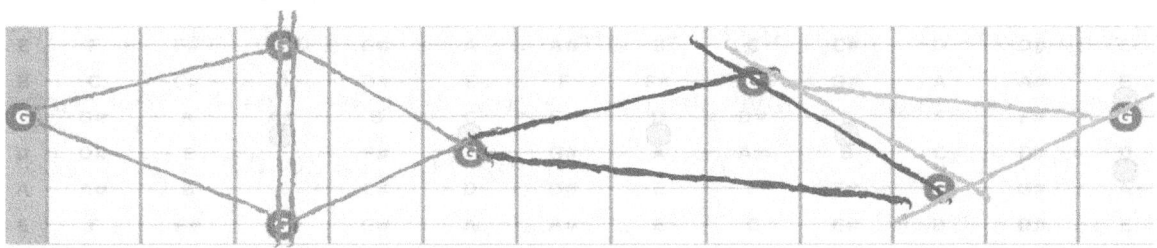

The same thing goes for the **fourth** and **second** strings. For example, if we have a note on the **fourth** string, you will be able to find that same note on the **second** string two strings up and three frets up. You can also use that note on the **fourth** string to find a note on the **fifth** string one string up and five frets up.

Your best bet is to break these triangular patterns down into individual clusters; you can separate them by color, if you'd like. The point of this exercise here is to see if you can form your own string and fret relationships with different root notes using the patterns that we have provided.

No matter the note you start on anywhere along the fretboard, you will be able to use these patterns to figure out where that same note exists on other strings. As you continue to go deeper into the world of guitar, you will be able to use these root patterns to help you figure out where certain notes exist within chords and scales. Overall, this will help you get your bearings along the fretboard.

We can't stress the importance of spatial awareness enough when it comes to memorizing the fretboard. The more you begin to internalize this idea, the easier it becomes to navigate the fretboard. Make sure to take these patterns and move them above the 12th fret to memorize the higher portion of the neck as well.

6.3 - Note Sequences

Note sequences allow you to develop the ability to visualize different arrangements of notes in various positions along the neck of the guitar. This *also* helps to increase your spatial awareness.

The idea is for you to create sequences of four or five notes, starting on the same root. Once you're comfortable with the sequences you've created, you should use a metronome to ground your time; you can also increase the speed while you play these. This exercise is a great workout or warm-up for your fingers!

You can either borrow these sequences from the scales you know, or you can simply pick out any series of notes.

These sequences can eventually evolve: instead of having the starting note on the root, you could start on any scale degree. But to keep it simple for now, we will use the root **G** as our starting note. Check out our sequences below:

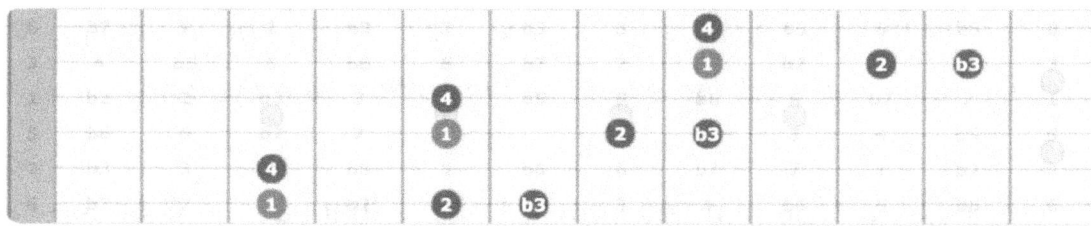

As you can see, the exercise above starts on the root, which is **G** in this case and moves to the **2** and **b3** on the same string before moving to the **4** on the next.

There are a few ways to use this exercise.

- For starters, and most obviously, it helps you to memorize where this sequence exists along the length of the neck in terms of notes.

- If you know that your root is **G**, then you should also know that two tones (whole-step) up from **G** is **A**. One step up from **A** is **A#/Bb**, and so on and so on. If you get to know this sequence really well, and then you use the above patterns to see where else this sequence exists, you can also figure out where the notes *within* the sequence exist.

Fun Fact:

This exercise helps with our auditory memorization. The brain is excellent at memorizing note patterns. It's one reason why we have the ability to sing back the chorus of a catchy song on the radio. If you spend enough time with it, the brain will recall the sound of this pattern when you need it.

Play the first sequence of notes from **1-4** above that has the **G** on the third fret of the low **E** string. Now play the second sequence of notes from **1-4** that has the **G** on the fifth fret of the **D** string.

Notice something?

They sound the same! The only difference is that the second sequence is one octave higher. By memorizing a series of notes in an auditory manner, you begin to develop an acute sense of patterns along the fretboard. This will eventually help you when it comes to improvisation or composition

Of course, the common reason that makes people choose to learn the notes of the fretboard is to enable them to move easily from one note to another when improvising. In our opinion, this is one of the best exercises to do so!

6.4 - Referencing the 12th Fret

When it comes to memorizing the fretboard, your brain will likely memorize some frets more quickly than others. The frets that we tend to grasp faster are the lower ones because they are closer to the open strings. Most guitarists are likely to have an easier time memorizing the notes on the lowest and highest strings. These tend to be easier to memorize because many of our chords and scales are often rooted in these strings.

Unfortunately, the middle strings don't get as much love as they deserve, which is often why guitarists find it more difficult to get a grasp of them.

This is why we recommend using the 12th fret reference exercise. The goal of this exercise is to get more comfortable with the frets that are closer to the 12th fret than the open string. Of course, the notes that come right after the 12th fret, such as the 12th-15th frets, are pretty easy to grasp; as we've mentioned, they simply act as a parallel to the area between the open string and 3rd fret.

What about the other frets in-between, though?

This is where referencing the 12th fret and counting backward can come in handy!

Let's say I wanted you to give me the name of the 8th fret on the **G** string, and there weren't any helpful references; after all, our anchor points are just out of reach! Your best bet would be to start on the natural note **G** at the 12th fret of the **G** string, shown above. You can then move backward fret by fret, in increments of semitones, until you get to the fret that you are looking for.

As you can see above, you count four semitones down from the natural note **G** to find the note **D#/Eb** on the eighth fret of the **G** string.

We highly recommend using this exercise when you are dealing with locating notes on the fretboard in areas where references are limited.

6.5 - Grouping Notes On The Fretboard

The idea of grouping notes on the fretboard is excellent for helping new guitarists remember string areas that aren't connected with a traditional chord or an open string. As you look at each group of notes, take it slow and practice playing the notes while saying them out loud as you pick them.

Practice playing these groupings both forward and backward.

After you have had all the natural note groups memorized, you can then begin adding your sharps and flats!

A-B-C

We will begin with the first three notes that can be found on the fifth string (**A**): **A-B-C**. Note how this grouping of notes is played with the same spacing between them on the sixth (**E**) string as well.

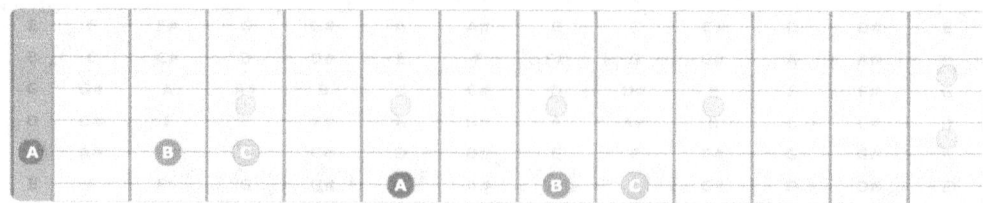

The idea is that wherever you find a natural note **A** on the fretboard, you will always know that a natural note **B** is a whole-step (tone) higher, and a natural note **C** is a half-step (semitone) higher than that.

The cool thing is that once you have the **A-B-C** on the open, second, and third frets of the **A** string memorized, you will also know that the *same* notes with the *same* pitch are found on the sixth (**E**) string!

C-D-E

The second note grouping is **C-D-E**. These three notes are a bit different because they are separated by whole-steps (tones). You will find **C-D-E** on the third, fifth, and seventh frets of the **A** string. You will also find **C-D-E** on the eighth, tenth, and twelfth frets of the sixth string (**E**).

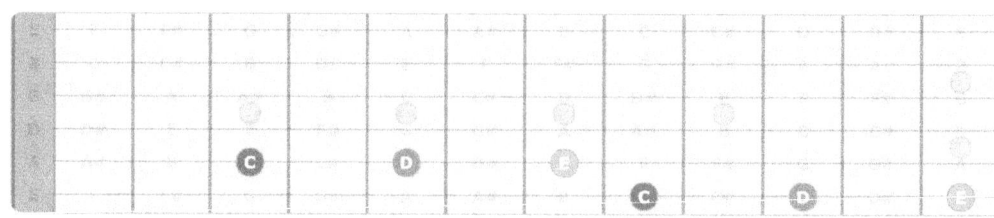

The idea is that whenever you find a **C** natural on the fretboard, you can move a whole-step (tone) up to find the **D** natural, then another whole-step up to find **E** natural. When moving backward, you can move a whole-step down from **E** to find **D**, then move another whole-step down to finish the note grouping on **C**!

E-F-G

The natural note grouping **E-F-G** can be found on the fifth string (**A**) and sixth string (**E**). This grouping can be found in the open position, on the first fret, and third fret of the sixth string (**E**), as well as the seventh fret, eighth fret, and tenth fret of the fifth string (**A**).

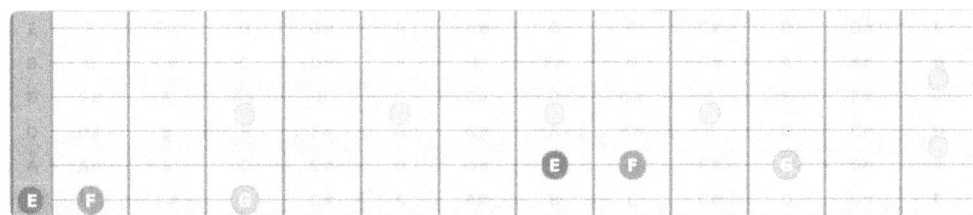

This grouping will have the same spacing anywhere on the fretboard: whenever you find a natural note **E**, you will find a natural note **F** a half-step (semitone) higher, and a natural note **G** a whole-step (tone) higher than that.

F-G-A

Finally, we have now reached our last natural note grouping, which is **F-G-A**. These notes are each separated by whole-steps, similar to **C-D-E**. When looking at the sixth string (**E**), you can find **F-G-A** on the first fret, third fret, and fifth fret. When looking at the fifth string (**A**), you can also find **F-G-A** on the eighth fret, tenth fret, and twelfth fret.

Whenever you find an **F** on the fretboard, you will find the note **G** a whole-step higher and an **A**, one whole-step higher than that. In reverse, if you find an **A** on the fretboard, you will find a **G** one whole-step down, and an **F** a whole-step down from that.

Remember to practice these notes slowly and *say each of them out loud* when playing them. Hold yourself accountable for the time you've put into this; test yourself! Grouping notes and finding patterns throughout the fretboard makes understanding the fretboard far less overwhelming.

6.6 - Two Additional Memorization Techniques

Lastly, we want to go over two easy techniques to help you memorize the notes on the fretboard by narrowing your focus. **1**: isolating one string at a time; **2**: isolating one note at a time.

Method One - One String At A Time

In this method, we will be looking at each of the strings as a separate entity instead of looking at the strings all at once, which can feel extremely overwhelming.

Look at the diagram below to see how you can begin practicing notes on the **high e** string:

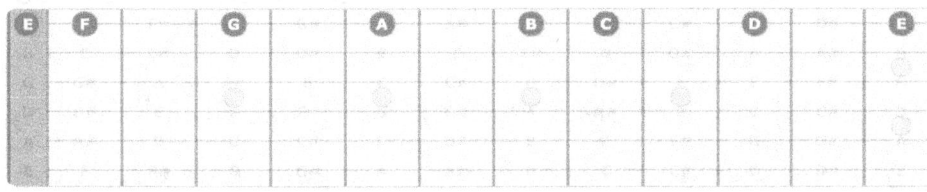

Notice how we only use the natural notes as we did earlier? There are no flats or sharps here.

This is because you can use what you know about tones and semitones to fill in these gaps mentally; moving up a semitone will give you the sharp version of these notes, and moving down a semitone will give you a flat version. In this stage, having an understanding of the natural notes is more important for us. Plus, it is much easier to memorize the position of eight notes rather than 12.

Remember, you can as well use this same pattern above the 12th fret! Once you have memorized this pattern on the high **E** string, you can move everything you've learned to the low **E** string, since they use the same note positions.

How To Practice With Method One

When using method one, start on the open **e** string and play one note at a time (following the notes on the diagram above) as you move up the length of the fretboard. Once you get to the twelfth fret, you can turn around and come back down using the same series of notes, though in reverse.

It is essential that you call the names of these notes out loud as you play them. As you are playing, say "**E, F, G**...." as you pluck each note. This is one of the best ways to supercharge the memorization process. You are essentially using multisensory integration by calling the names of the notes out loud.

Yes, it might feel a little odd saying notes out loud at first, but it will help you gain a better understanding of the fretboard **much** faster compared to doing this silently. *It is easy to just memorize the frets to play, but it is essential to know the notes, too!*

Here are some of the top tips to remember when using method one:

- Take the exercise slowly. You never want to rush through any of these exercises. Going slow allows time for your brain to process the notes as you play them so that they all sink into your memory better. Take it easy and speed up as you get better. We highly recommend playing along with a metronome as you get more comfortable with the notes.
- Keep your focus strong. Make sure to focus on each note's name and position as you run through all the notes. Focus on your breath, and take short breaks when you need to.
- Don't overstress the finger that you use in playing the notes. If you want to play all the notes with your index finger, that is totally fine. The focus here should be the names of the notes, not the technique you use in playing them!
- As you progress, make it a point to focus on the areas that you are not feeling very confident with. Practicing the guitar should *always* be about turning your weaknesses into strengths.

The first few times that you play through any exercise, it might feel incredibly daunting and you may be surprised at how slow you are going.

That is how it should feel! It happens to the best musicians out there. This means that you are progressing, believe it or not.

If you are getting frustrated or feel that the exercise is difficult, then take a deep breath, be patient, and keep on moving. We promise that over the next couple of days, you will find out that the exercises would become surprisingly easier. Before you know it, you'll be able to hit the positions and name the notes in a pinch. Your playing will get faster, and you won't get stuck in the weak areas that you got stuck in before.

Here is the same exercise on the **G** string:

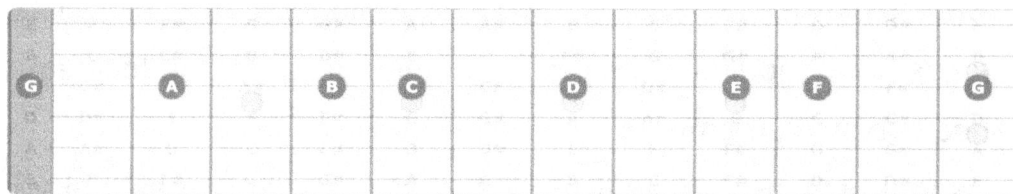

You can as well follow the exact same method that you did on the **E** string. Call the notes out loud as you get to each position. We *also* recommend naming the frets:

"Second fret: **A**; Fourth fret: **B**; Fifth fret: **C**……"

The more specific you are with your focus, the more beneficial these exercises will be for you.

We recommend that you should only practice one string for a whole week before moving on to the next one. This way, you will be sure to ingrain each string into your memory before trying to give your brain something new. Try integrating it into part of your practice routine.

Why We Love This Method

This method is awesome because it allows you to think in a **linear** manner. Instead of trying to memorize the shape or position of a scale, you can think about how the notes on certain strings connect together. Though it could also be a fun exercise in music theory to find out the scales, or modes, these exercises form!

You begin to take in certain contextual positions, such that **"D** will always be a whole-step up from **C"** or that "**F** will always be a half-step up from **E"** no matter the string you are playing on.

When improvising in the future, you will always have an idea of where certain notes are from your current position.

Furthermore, since you are practicing one string at a time, you won't develop any weak areas along the length of the fretboard. There are many guitarists out there that don't feel 100% comfortable with certain areas on the fretboard. This is because there are a lot of shapes and patterns that focus on specific areas than others.

When you master this method, you will gain confidence throughout the entirety of the fretboard.

Method Two - One Note At A Time

Method One can help us locate notes as we move up and down the strings individually. Although method one is a very useful tool, we're not always going to be playing up and down single strings. We eventually want to be able to hop from one string to the next.

Method Two comes as a supplement to Method One to help us fill in any gaps that we're left with.

Method Two is going to feel a bit more difficult compared to Method One right off the bat, as it is a completely different exercise. It is very effective because it keeps your fretboard geography honest: It allows you to memorize notes in a way that almost makes it impossible to cheat.

After mastering Method Two, you will be able to find any note on the fretboard within an instant. Method Two works to help guitarists memorize the positions of specific notes across the fretboard without needing any reference points.

Earlier, we talked about the twelfth fret and how it can be used as a reference to find specific notes on the fretboard. If you are trying to find the note **G** on the **B** string, you might think that "the 12th fret of the **B** string is the natural note **B**, and **G** is four semi-tones down from **B**, which means that **G** is on the eighth fret of the **B** string."

While the 12th fret reference method is awesome, Method Two will allow you to find the **G** on the eighth fret of the **B** string (or 19th fret of the **B** string) instantly.

Here is how we use Method Two:

- **Pick A Note That You Want To Find:** We want to narrow our focus to one note at a time. Remember, the main goal of this exercise is to find where a note lives in various positions across the entirety of the fretboard. Choose any musical note.
- **Locate Your Chosen Note On The Low E String,** *(below The 12th Fret)*: As we have mentioned earlier, every string runs a full octave from the open position up to the twelfth fret. This means that, in that octave range, we will find every note on every string once. The exception is that we will find the note twice if your note is the open string, as it will also be found on the twelfth fret. Locate your note as quickly as possible and pluck it while saying it out loud.
- **Next, Move To The A String:** Here, you will simply have to do the same thing. Find where that same note is on the **A** string, and say it out loud as you pluck it.

- **Continue Across The Strings:** Every time you have located your note on one string, move one string up, and repeat the entire process. Once you have gone through all the strings, move down from the **high e** string and do the exercise in reverse.
- **Repeat With Different Notes:** Once you have one note down, work your way through all of the notes. Let's assume that you start with the natural note **E**. Next, you could move to the natural note **F**, then **F#/Gb,** and so on.

This method is incredibly simple when you think about it, even though it might feel a bit odd at first. The cool thing is that it completely removes the idea of pattern or shape memorization from the equation.

Of course, it is essential to do this exercise properly. When locating a note, try not to think of things like, "**A** must be on this fret because I just found **G**, and **A** is always two frets up from **G**."

Although that thought process can be helpful, it will actually hurt our progress for this particular exercise. To prevent that type of "crutch," try writing down the notes on flashcards and picking them at random, or use any creative way to randomly generate letters. This will help your fretboard geography greatly.

How To Practice With Method Two

Let's begin by looking at an example of how we can use Method Two in our practice routines.

Look at the fretboard below, and you will see the natural note **G** across all the strings, from the open position to the twelfth fret:

As you can see from the diagram above, **G** appears only once on every string, except for the **G** string, where it appears once as the open string and once on the twelfth fret.

With practice, you will be able to find all the natural **G** notes quickly without needing to refer to any other positions. Even if you are visualizing shapes and patterns subconsciously from what we learned earlier, try to block that out for now.

You can skip the open string if you want and just play the **G** on the twelfth fret, as there is a chance that you already have the open strings ingrained into your memory.

Once you're done with **G,** you can then move on to a new note. We recommend starting with notes that have open string names, then all-natural notes, and then the notes with accidentals. In this case, we will jump ahead; let's assume that the new note is **G#/Ab:**

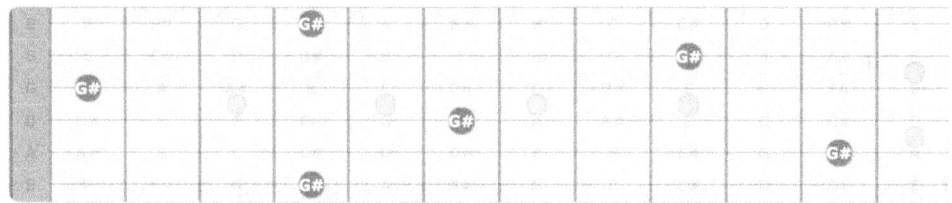

The cool thing about trying to attack notes with accidentals is that they will be inevitably harder. The whole point of this exercise is to give you a good idea of where your weak areas lie when looking for notes. It also removes the idea of using memorized shapes and patterns from the equation. If you find out that one note is extremely easy to memorize and that another note is difficult, then you can use this exercise to get that difficult note up to speed.

Here is how we suggest using Method Two:

- **Listen Carefully:** When you play a note on one string and move up to find that same note on the next string, it should sound like the same note. If you hit a wrong note, it will sound pretty obvious. Playing a **G#**, for example, when you are looking to play **G**, will sound "off" and dissonant.
- **Notice Octaves**: Sometimes when we jump from one string to the next, those two notes will sound *exactly* the same in pitch: when playing the example above, notice the sound of the **G#** on the **D** string, and the sound of the **G#** on the **G** string; they should sound like the same note. Sometimes when we jump from one string to the next, the

notes will sound an *octave apart*: using the above example, you will notice how the sound of the **G#** on the **D** string and the **G#** on the **B** string have that octave sound. Pay close attention to where these octaves exist, as it will help you out when you get into improvisation a little down the line.

- **Say Your Note Names Aloud:** As we said earlier, saying your notes out loud is incredibly helpful. You can think of it as another way to burn these notes into your memory.
- **Keep Track Of Your Time:** One of the best ways to see yourself grow is to time yourself. See how fast you can get through each note. As you do this exercise throughout the week, you will be able to see yourself progressing. In addition, you will also be able to pinpoint any weak areas that you might have: one note may take you twice as long compared to another.

Keep practicing this method, and we promise that you will begin to feel extremely confident when it comes to your knowledge of the fretboard!

Chapter 7: Practice Routine Ideas

Using a Practice Journal

As of now, you have plenty of cool exercises sitting in front of you.

You might be asking,

How can I implement all of these?

It's important to create a routine for yourself! A routine can help you stay on track as you practice to memorize the fretboard effectively.

Of course, there are many different ways you could use the above exercises, and you do not necessarily *have* to follow **our** practice routine. You can also feel free to make yours if you feel that it would be more helpful.

However, we know how much musicians like to be given structure when it comes to practice, so that's what we are going to provide!

Here is our 5-Day Memorization Routine:

Pro Tip - Use a stopwatch or timer with all of these exercises. This will help to stimulate positive pressure so that you can see where you are and grow each day.

Day 1 - Octaves:

Before we dive in, we want to preface this section with a quick warning: you shouldn't be putting a lot of pressure on yourself right off the bat. If you can give yourself *at least* 5-10 minutes of memorization practice during your daily practice routine, that would be enough to allow you to make progress daily! Fretboard memorization is all about the "long game," consistent practice over time, which serves as the key to truly learning this material.

We find that it is best to focus on one thing at a time, which is why we will start with **Octaves.**

Here is what you might expect from a 5-10 minute octave practice routine:
- Pick a note on your low **E** string: for this example, we will pick the natural note **F** on the first fret of the **E** string.
- From that **F**, find where the **F** is on the fifth string.
- Move to the fourth string, the third string, the second string, and the final sixth string, finding the note **F** on all of them.
- Pick another random note and repeat the process; as we've suggested with other exercises, pick natural notes for this process

first, and as you get more comfortable, you can then add sharps and flats.

Day 2 - Root Patterns:

Next, let's hop into **Root Patterns**

Here is what you might practice in a 5-10 minute root pattern routine:

- Start with the root **G**. We always recommend starting with the root **G**, as it is a commonly used root on the guitar.
- Start with **G** on the sixth string (low **E**) and find all of your reachable octaves from that **G** using the octave patterns that we learned in chapter 5. Start with our closest octave—up two strings, up two frets—then play all other **G**'s within reaching distance.
- Once you have found the octave from the **G** on the sixth (**E**) string, burn those patterns into your brain.
- Next, move your root to a higher or lower note on the sixth string (low **E**). We would recommend skipping around to make things more challenging, instead of moving down to **Gb** or up to **G#.**
- Once you feel comfortable with your roots from the sixth string (**E**), you can move on to the fifth string (**A**) and repeat the same steps.
- From there, move on to each string and repeat the process.

Day 3 - Note Groupings

We went over the idea of grouping notes back in Chapter 6. It's a great way to understand note combinations that aren't typically part of regular chords or open strings. Here is how you can practice note groupings:

- For the note grouping exercise, we recommend starting with the natural notes **A-B-C**.
- Find your **A-B-C** pattern on the sixth string (low **E**) using your knowledge of the bottom string.
- Next, move on to the fifth string (**A**) and find the same **A-B-C** pattern.
- You can continue moving on to the fourth (**D**), third (**G**), second (**B**), and first (**e**) strings, finding where the **A-B-C** pattern lies on all of them. *Finding this pattern on the **B** string is a little tricky; since B is the lowest possible note on this string, you can't use it in this sequence. Therefore, you will have to use the 12th fret octave instead. See if you can figure it out, and always remember that the fretboard mirrors itself after the 12th fret.*
- Once you have found the pattern on each string, play through all of them in succession, starting from the sixth (**E**) string all the way down to the first (**e**) string, and back. You can even set up a metronome for yourself to see how accurate you can get through all of them; it's easy to slow down when changing strings, or rush! This doubles as an accuracy exercise and warm-up exercise!

- From there, move on to your other natural note patterns, including **C-D-E**, **E-F-G,** and **F-G-A**, thus repeating all the same steps.

Day 4 – Method One: One String at a Time

On the fourth day, we will switch gears a bit and hit Method One, the "One String at a Time" approach. There are a few ways that you can practice Method One, though this is how we believe it works best:

- Start on the sixth string (low **E**) and play up and down the entire string from the open position to the highest fret, including sharps and flats, while calling the names out loud. Do this ascending and descending 5 times. When ascending, call out the sharp names (**E, F, F#, G, G#,** etc.); when descending, call out the flat names (**Ab, G, Gb, F, E**).
- Move to the fifth string (**A**) and repeat the same steps.
- Continue moving down the face of the fretboard to the highest string (high **e**).

Be patient with yourself! This might seem daunting at first, but we promise that it will help you to create a visual memory of each string. It also helps that the musical alphabet only has 12 different notes to remember, and they will continue to follow each other, string to string. *Imagine if each string had its own set of 12 different notes, that would be 72 different notes! Thankfully, we only need to memorize our 12 notes from the chromatic scale.*

It's a wonderful way to get started because you get to spend a bit of time on each of the strings before moving on to the next. We also recommend using a metronome, as this exercise can *also* double as an accuracy exercise! Make sure to start slow; don't pick up the pace until you're comfortable with the slower tempo. It won't matter how fast the exercise is played if it's sloppy!

You can write down your metronome speed (beats per minute) and measure your progress from week to week to track your growth! From there, we can move on to Method two.

Day 5 - Method Two: One Note at a Time

Once you feel comfortable with Method One, you can move on to Method Two, which is the "One Note at a Time" approach. Here's how we recommend using it in a practice routine:

- Let's use the note **A** as our starting point.
- Moving from the lowest string to the highest string, one at a time, find each **A**. For this exercise, we only want to work below the 12th fret. You can move this exercise above the 12th fret once you are done, but for the sake of keeping things simple, let's keep it below for now.
- Start this exercise very slowly. You can use a metronome and speed it up as you move along, but make sure that you are calling the name of the note out loud every time you pluck it.

- Once you feel comfortable with **A**, you can move on to the next natural note, **B,** thereby going through the steps again.
- Continue working through the musical alphabet from **A-G,** using all the steps listed above.
- Add your accidentals! When you are comfortable with this exercise using all the natural notes, try going through the process while adding flats and sharps.

As you practice, observe the notes that *you* feel least comfortable with. Let's assume that you struggled more with finding **C#** on every string compared to others. In that case, write down **C#** in your practice journal so that you will be aware that you will need to practice it next time.

Chapter 8: Conclusion

Congratulations!

You have just completed the fretboard memorization book!

All the information and exercises in this book were made to help you grasp the note positions on the fretboard. Of course, you must follow them diligently.

Developing visual coordination and spatial awareness is a **MAJOR** part of becoming a confident guitarist. Whether you are looking to improvise on stage, write your own songs, or just have fun playing at home, having a deep understanding of the fretboard is very helpful.

Overall, memorizing the fretboard will keep you from ever feeling stranded in certain neck positions. You'll always have multiple bearings or starting points that you will be able to navigate with. Furthermore, the more you practice, the more comfortable you will be able to navigate through the different positions of the guitar neck.

Thanks for reading, and we wish you luck on your guitar journey moving forward!

www.ingramcontent.com/pod-product-compliance
Lightning Source LLC
Chambersburg PA
CBHW081755100526
44592CB00015B/2447